AROMAS OF INDIA

A HISTORICAL AND CULTURAL OVERVIEW OF INDIA'S SPICE TRADE

DR. JAGADEESH PILLAI

Made with ❤ on the Notion Press Platform
www.notionpress.com

|| "Dedicated to all who seek to understand and appreciate Indian culture and tradition." ||

Contents

Contents

PRAYER

"Om Bhadram Karnebhih Shrunuyaama DevaahBhadram Pashyemaakshabhiryajatraah SthirairangaistushtuvaamsastanoobhihVyashema Devahitam YadaayuhSwasti Na Indro VridhashravaahSwasti Nah Pooshaa VishwavedaahSwasti Nastaarkshyo ArishtanemihSwasti No Brihaspatir DadhaatuOm Shantih, Shantih, Shantih"

The literal meaning of this mantra is: OM. O Gods! Let us hear auspicious words from our ears. O reverent Gods! Let us behold propitious visions from our eyes, let our organs and body be stable, healthy, and strong. Let us do that which is pleasing to the gods in the life span allotted to us. May Indra, inscribed in the scriptures, bring us fortune! May Pushan, the knower of the world, grant us prosperity! May Trakshya, who vanquishes enemies, bestow us with blessings! May Brihaspati bring us success!
OM Peace, Peace, Peace.

About The Author

Dr. Jagadeesh Pillai is a renowned Guinness World Record holder, writer, and researcher hailing from Varanasi, also known as the abode of Lord Shiva. With a Ph.D. in Vedic Science and a range of creative ideas and achievements, he is a true polymath. He is the author of more than 100 books including Research Publications. Although his roots can be traced back to Kerala, the people of Varanasi hold him in high regard and affectionately consider him one of their own.

Dr. Pillai has achieved four Guinness World Records in the following subjects:

"Script to Screen" - In this record, Dr. Pillai produced and directed an animation film within the shortest time possible, breaking the previous record set by Canadians. He has also received numerous national and international awards and recognitions for this achievement.

Longest Line of Postcards - For this record, Dr. Pillai created a line of 16,300 postcards on the occasion of the 163rd anniversary of Indian Postal Day. The event also included a questionnaire about the Indian flag.

Largest Poster Awareness Campaign - Dr. Pillai designed an awareness campaign on the subject of "Beti Bachao - Beti Padhao" (Save the Girl Child - Educate the Girl Child) to achieve this record.

Largest Envelope - In tribute to the Indian Prime Minister's

"Make in India" initiative, Dr. Pillai created a 4000 square meter envelope using waste paper to achieve this record.

Attempted - **70000 Candles on a 210 kg Cake** - To celebrate the 70th Indian Independence Day, Dr. Pillai attempted to light 70,000 candles on a 210 kg cake, which was recorded in World Records India.

Attempted - **Documentary on Dhamek Stupa of Sarnath in 17 Languages** - Dr. Pillai attempted to create a documentary on the Dhamek Stupa of Sarnath, dubbing it in 17 different languages. The result of this attempt is currently awaiting confirmation from the Guinness World Records.

Dr. Pillai is skilled in teaching the Bhagavad Gita, a Hindu scripture, and is popular among young people. He has helped many young people improve their lives through his motivational teachings.

In addition to teaching, he has composed and sung numerous Sanskrit Bhajans and patriotic songs.

He has also written and directed several short films and documentaries for awareness campaigns, and has volunteered with the police in both UP and Kerala to spread awareness about various issues through videos and photography.

Incredibly, he has produced and directed over 100 documentaries about the city of Varanasi, all on his own.

He has also helped and guided more than 25 boys and girls to achieve world records through creative and innovative methods. He is a multifaceted person who uses his intellect and the blessings given to him by God to excel in various areas. He is both a teacher and a student, always learning and teaching, and is able to master any subject he comes across.

He is a selfless social activist and motivational speaker who has overcome struggles and failures to become a successful and enthusiastic individual with a rich life experience.

In addition to his work with the Bhagavad Gita, he is also an efficient Tarot card reader, Astro-Vastu consultant, and a talented singer and composer. He has sung the entire Ram Charita Manas and Bhagavad Gita in his own compositions, and has sung the phrase "Lokah Samastha Sukhino Bhavantu" in 50 different languages. He is currently working on a detailed and scientific study of Vedas, Upanishads, Puranas, and the Bhagavad Gita. He has also composed and sung the Hanuman Chalisa and Gayatri Mantra in 108 and 1008 different compositions, respectively.

Awards - Four Times Guinness World Records, Winner of Mahatma Gandhi Vishwa Shanti Puraskar, Mahatma Gandhi Global Peace Ambassador, Kashi Ratna Award, Dr. APJ Abdul Kalam Motivational Person of the Year 2017, Mother Teresa Award, Indira Gandhi Priyadarshini Award, Bharat Vikas Ratna Award, Udyog Ratna Award, Vigyan Prasar Award, Poorvanchal Ratn Samman.

Preface

The Indian spice trade is a fascinating and complex phenomenon with a long and varied history. For centuries, spices have been a source of wealth and a symbol of power, with traders travelling vast distances to bring their wares to faraway markets. This book, The Indian Spice Trade: A Historical and Cultural Overview of India's Spice Trade, seeks to explore the history, culture, and significance of the Indian spice trade.

This book is intended to serve as an introduction to the rich history and culture of the Indian spice trade for readers who are new to the subject. It explores the ancient spice routes, the spice trade in the Roman era, and the medieval spice trade. It also examines India's role as the nexus of international trade, the significance of spices, the Portuguese exploration of India, the rise of globalisation, and the impact of climate change on the Indian spice trade.

The book draws on research from a variety of sources, including interviews with key figures in the Indian spice trade industry, archival materials, and cultural analysis. I have also conducted extensive field research in India, including attending spice festivals, interviewing spice traders, and visiting locations associated with the production of spices. Through this research, I hope to provide readers with a comprehensive understanding of the Indian spice trade industry and its various components.

I am deeply passionate about the art of the Indian spice trade and hope that this book will help to spread the appreciation of this wonderful form of commerce. I believe that the Indian spice trade has a great deal to offer to the world and I am excited to share its cultural and historical significance with my readers.

I

Introduction to the Indian Spice Trade history & cultural overview

The Indian spice trade is one of the oldest and most profitable trades in the world. It is a fascinating story that goes back thousands of years, and today, India remains one of the world's main producers of many aromatic and flavor-rich spices.

The earliest evidence of an Indian spice trade dates back to some three thousand years ago. This was when merchants travelling the ancient world would carry with them many spices and herbs, including cinnamon, turmeric, coriander, ginger, pepper, cardamom and others, to be traded with distant lands such as Egypt, Persia, Greece, and Rome. Even as early as at this point, the Indian spices were highly sought after, and were even sometimes exchanged for gold or other valuable commodities. The trade in Indian spices was further legitimized with the opening of the Spice Route, which was an ancient network of trade routes that connected the Indian subcontinent and the Mediterranean region.

In the medieval era, Indian spices were particularly valuable, and highly sought after in Europe, where there was little else that could be used to flavor food. Spices from India such as saffron, pepper, turmeric and cinnamon, were exported to Europe and its colonies in large quantities, and in turn, Indian merchants would bring back valuable trade goods from the West.

Today, the Indian spice trade is still very much in existence, with India being one of the largest exporters of spices in the world. India stands for a fifth of the global spice market, and dominates the market in various countries. Most of the spices from India are exported to other Asian countries, Europe and the United States, and India is an especially important trading partner to developed countries in the region.

Apart from the commercial aspect of Indian spice trading, the cultural aspects of it are also immense. Indian spices form a major part of the Indian cuisine, and carry with them a long and deep-rooted history. The preparation of food and the various methods of drying, grinding and combining different spices, serves as the foundation of Indian cuisine and culture today.

In short, the Indian spice trade is and has been a major

feature in India for thousands of years. It is a trade that demonstrates the power of spices, of commerce between nations and of the culinary culture that has influenced entire nations. In many ways, it serves as a reminder of one of the oldest trades in the world and of the incredible impact it has had over the centuries and even to this day.

"The aroma of spices has been a symbol of India's heritage and diversity."

II

The Ancient Spice Routes

The Indian spice trade has been a major force in commerce and culture since antiquity. Spices were one of the earliest trading commodities and were used to bring flavor and aroma to dishes, but also had many other uses, such as medicine and cosmetics. In ancient times, the demand for these commodities extended far beyond the Indian subcontinent. This created an entire network of trading routes known as the Spice Routes, which were exchanged between the Western and Eastern worlds, as well as between Indian states and countries of the Middle East and Far East.

The first known Trade route between Asia and Europe was established in the 4th century BC, when the Greeks and Romans began trading with the Indian subcontinent. During this period, traders from the Middle East and Far East transported spices from Gujarat and Kerala, India, to the Mediterranean and European regions. This early form of international trade fostered the growth of both Indian and foreign civilizations; spices became an important part of both everyday and special occasions. This in turn helped the Indian economy to flourish and led to an increase in mercantile activity, particularly along the spices route.

The Indian spice trade continued to develop during the Middle Ages, when trade routes and caravans further facilitated the movement of goods from one country to another. By the 11th century, the sea routes from India to Southeast Asia, particularly to the major cities of China, were well established, allowing for large cargoes of spices to be moved from the Indian subcontinent to the area of the Spice Islands. This facilitated the spread of Indian spices to the East and to European countries, which consequently led to an increase in their demand.

As the Indian spice trade rose in prominence, more merchants entered the market and the trade routes became even more extensive. This spurred the creation of a global spice trade network, which stretched from Europe, through Turkey, to the cities of Syria, Arabia, and Egypt. From there, spices traveled further to India, where they were then shipped to ports in the Far East, such as Malacca, China, Thailand and Cambodia. This primarily involved the transportation of goods by land and sea, and also included the use of camels and mules to transport goods over the desert.

The spice trade remained a major factor in the Indian economy until the early 19th century when it began to decline, due to the industrialization of Europe and the opening of new trade routes around the world. Although the demand for spices has decreased, the trade routes that have existed for centuries continue to play an important role in the global economy. The Spice Routes also remain an intriguing part of the world's history, providing insight into the importance of early Indian trade and its impact on other countries.

"The spice trade has played a vital role in shaping India's economy and society."

ꕥ

III

The Spice Trade in the Roman Era

The Roman spice trade was a lucrative and important part of commerce in both the Ancient Roman Empire and its eventual successor, the Byzantine Empire that lasted from the 1st to the 15th century. Although the Romans were not the first to trade in spices and other exotic goods, they were able to use their superior engineering abilities and military power to make the trade more efficient and lucrative.

The Mediterranean region was at the heart of the early Roman spice trade. Through the port city of Ostia and its network of imperial roads, merchants across the Mediterranean came to purchase valuable spices and other luxury goods from Arab merchants and later from the silk road. Not only was Rome an important center for trade, but it also received goods from other lands such as India, as well as African and Asian markets, providing an important source of wealth for the empire's citizens.

Spices such as pepper, cloves, cardamom, frankincense and others were highly sought after in ancient Rome. Many of these spices had medicinal benefits and were used to treat a variety of ailments. In addition, they were also used to preserve food and give it a special flavor and appeal. This was especially important during the summer months when it was difficult to keep food fresh.

The Roman Empire developed a trade network to ensure regular and uninterrupted supply of spices to its many markets. To do this, they employed agents located in cities such as Alexandria and Damascus to purchase spices at various ports and direct them toward Rome. These agents eventually developed their own trade routes, known as the Indian Maritime Spice Routes, to help reduce the cost of transporting goods to Rome.

Due to the high demand for spices, their costs increased with the rise of the empire. This caused prices to be out of reach for most common citizens, and those of the poorer classes had to substitute domestic spices such as cumin and oregano instead. The wealthy, however, continued to use exotic spices, as they believed them to be a sign of refinement, status and wealth.

The Roman spice trade played an important role throughout the empire, providing a steady supply of valuable goods that had both a practical and social use. The wealth and influence of the Roman Empire was largely dependent on the availability and accessibility of these spices, and they remain an important symbol of the empire's history even today.

"From the Malabar Coast to the World, Indian spices have been a source of wealth and prosperity."

☙

IV

The Medieval Spice Trade

The Indian Spice Trade was a cornerstone of the global economy during the Middle Ages, with vast amounts of spices, such as cardamom, black pepper, and cumin, moving across the world and fetching valuable prices. The spice trade flourished due to a host of factors, ranging from the geographic position of India, both in terms of trade routes and its natural resources, to the evolving tastes of European consumers and the strength of the Indian merchants.

India was ideally situated to become a major player in the spice trade, due to its geographic location connecting the East and West. Through its spice-producing regions—including the western coastal region and the Western Ghats mountain range, which were still known as the "Malabar Coast" in the Middle Ages—India had access to the Persian Gulf, the Arabian Sea, and beyond. In addition,

India's much-lauded monsoon winds enabled ships to travel from Western India to the trade entrepôts of Egypt, the Middle East, and even Europe, carrying spices along the way.

At the same time, Indian merchants were well-positioned to reap the benefits of this trade. With a strong presence in the international market, Indian spices such as black pepper, cumin, and cardamom were much sought after in all the major trading posts. In fact, the trade in spices became synonymous with Indian trade, and Indian merchants played a major role in the transfer of spices from producer to consumer.

This trade was further strengthened by the emergence of a new consumer culture in Europe during the Middle Ages. As Europeans began to explore the world beyond their own borders, they gained access to spices that were unfamiliar, yet highly desirable. The popularity of spices increased significantly, and Indian merchants seized this opportunity to obtain large sums of money by supplying these highly sought-after spices abroad.

The Indian Spice Trade was one of the cornerstones of the global economy during the Middle Ages. Its success was a testament to the strength of Indian merchants, the geographic advantages of India, and the new consumer culture that had developed in Europe. This trade resulted in fortunes being made in both India and abroad through the exchange of spices, profits that have lasted even until today.

"The spice trade has been a bridge between East and West, connecting cultures and civilizations."

ꟼꟼ

V

India as the Nexus of International Trade

India has a rich history of global commerce, with trade networks stretching from the Mediterranean to Southeast Asia. The Indian subcontinent has long served as a nexus of international exchange, particularly in the realm of spices. Since antiquity, India has acted as a hub of spice production and trade, providing high-quality products to countries all over the world.

A vast variety of fragrant and flavorful spice products emanate from India. Alliums like garlic and ginger, aromatics like cardamom and cinnamon, and floral flavors like lavender and rose petals can be found in abundance in India. Throughout the centuries, merchants have journeyed to the subcontinent to buy and export these precious spices, which were held in high regard by many foreign cultures.

The ancient Egyptians worked with Indian merchants in supplying spices to the Mediterranean, while Silk Road traders used Indian spices to sweeten the dishes of China and Japan.

In addition to these established trading routes, India also took part in extensive maritime trade with Europe. European merchants established trading posts in India and the rest of the subcontinent, beginning the process of trading spices to Western countries. Demand was high not just in Europe, but also in the Middle East, thanks to Indian spices' reputation for being potent and flavorful. The age of sail saw even more widespread trade, as merchants from Europe and beyond traveled to India's shores to enjoy the abundant supply of spices.

By the 19th century, India had become firmly entrenched as the preeminent source of high-quality spices for the global market. India was producing many of the world's most prized spices, including pepper, cardamom, nutmeg, and turmeric. The country's vast population meant that its producers could easily supply large quantities of the sought-after commodities, while its strategic location and long trading history gave its products a certain level of prestige.

Today, India continues to be one of the world's foremost spice producers and maintain its place as the nexus of international spice trade. As a result, Indian spices are becoming more and more popular around the world, with the country's products being sought after in both traditional and modern kitchens. The Indian spices that are available today are just as high-quality and flavorful as they were centuries ago, and their flavor continues to be cherished around the world.

"India's spices have been a source of inspiration for art, literature and cuisine"

ꝏ

VI

The Significance of Spices

For centuries, spices have been used not only as integral ingredients in recipes but also for trading. India, at the heart of the world's spice trade, has been supplying spices for centuries. The Indian Spice Trade not only shaped the economy of India and its neighboring countries, but also revolutionized the way of trading around the world. This established trade revolutionized the way the Western world understands food.

India's spice production and trade has a long and fascinating history, starting with the ancient civilizations that flourished in the area around 1500 BC. By 300 BC Sri Lankan traders started to transport spices eastward across the Indian Ocean. By the 1st century CE, merchants began buying and selling spices through silent bartering and the demand for spices soon spread to Ancient China and Egypt. During the medieval ages, most of the world's spices originated from India and it was a powerful trading point for its neighboring countries like China and Egypt.

The importance of the Indian Spice Trade was undeniable. Spices served many purposes ranging from medicinal purposes, religious purposes and for flavoring food. The popularity of spices led to increased trade as spices were used for embalming in Egypt and for aromatization in Greece. Later, spices were exported to the West for consumption and for trade with Europe. As a result, traders from all over the world traveled to India to buy and sell spices, establishing it as the center of the spice market.

The Indian Spice Trade also played a role in medical warfare. Clove oil, cayenne pepper and turmeric were used to heal wounds, while others were utilized to make dangerous weapons fireproof. Famous explorers like Vasco da Gama, Jackie Kennedy and Christopher Columbus even ventured to India to trade spices.

The Indian Spice Trade ushered in a new era of culinary knowledge that created an immense impact on the economy, the way of life and the culture. It gave spices a wider appreciation and newfound respect because of their essential contributions to cuisines worldwide. Today, food without spices is near-impossible and we owe our modern palates to the Indian Spice Trade. Spices are still an integral part of India today, and their long trading history stands as a testament to the significant impact it has had on the world.

"The spice trade has been a reflection of India's creativity and innovation"

VII

The Portuguese Exploration of India

The Portuguese exploration of India is an indispensable part of the Indian history and is an indefinite milestone in the modern world system. To explore India, the Portuguese found several sea routes and sought to trade in goods from the eastern world. When the Portuguese arrived in India, spicess were in great demand in Europe; this fact encouraged the Portuguese to engage in a wildly successful Indian Spice Trade.

After the establishment of the Vasco da Gama-led Portuguese colony in India in 1510, the Portuguese began to control the spice trade, which had already been operated by the Arabs, Indians, and the Venetians. Through this, the Portuguese Empire gradually strengthened its hold on India's spice market. During their rule, the Portuguese focused on making a profit from their monopoly on the Indian spice trade. They were able to use their influence from Europe to gain a competitive edge in the market and put pressure on the indigenous trading company.

The Portuguese played an integral role in the discovery and spread of previously unknown spices throughout Europe. These spices would later transform the culinary culture and diet in many countries. The most valuable spices explored by the Portuguese included pepper, nutmeg, cloves, cardamom, and cinnamon. When talking about the value of spices, it's important to mention that Indian pepper became the first truly global commodity with impacts across the globe.

Apart from the spice trade, the Portuguese in India brought a cultural exchange. The contacts between the local rulers and the Portuguese involved intermarriage and close ties. The Portuguese brought with them Christianity and its related customs, beliefs, and expressions that were new to Indian people.

The Portuguese discovery and involvement with Indian spice trade had a lasting impact, not only on the cultural aspects, but also on the economic development of the world. Their methods of exploration eventually helped to create international fleets, which were key in the beginnings of the Global economy.

The Portuguese exploration of India was truly a historic event, making a great and permanent impact in the Indian culture and economy. The Portuguese were thefirst Europeans to travel to India and spread the knowledge of previously unknown spices. They encouraged the expansion of world trade and help start the globalization process. Thus, it is only natural to recognize the Portuguese exploration of India for its essential part in shaping India's history and its impacts on the modern world.

"The spice trade has been a route to India's spiritual and cultural heritage"

VIII

The Rise of Globalisation

Spices have been considered a valuable commodity throughout history, with some of the earliest trade routes being established for the sole purpose of exchanging spices from one country to another. For centuries, India has been a major centre for the production of many of the world's most beloved spices. From the humble peppercorn to the exotic cardamom, the spice trade has long been an integral part of India's development, rising to become a prominent player in the globalisation of the world's economy.

In the pre-modern period, Indian spices were among the first goods to be traded in international commerce. Monarchs and merchants alike recognised the value in spices and recognised the potential profits to be made by establishing trading routes. Indian goods and goods from the Far East were exchanged through vast networks of merchant ships, military vessels, and traditional caravans.

This activity gave rise to the concept of the Spice Route, and it was through this route that India was able to become a leader in the spice trade.

The East India Company played a major role in the spread of Indian spices across the globe. Established in 1600, the company dealt heavily in the trade and production of spices, impacting India's role in globalisation. During the colonial period, Indian spice traders were able to capitalize on the demand for their goods, leading to increased production and improvements in their production methods. The company invested heavily in the infrastructure of the spice trade and aided in the expansion of the route, making it easier and more efficient to export spices to other countries.

This rise in international trade enhanced India's influence on the world's economy. Countries in Europe, the Middle East and Asia began to rely on India as their primary supplier of spices and as such Indian traders quickly became integral to the globalisation of the world's economy. This dependence on India for spices allowed traders to raise prices, resulting in increased profits.

Over the course of centuries, the Indian spice trade rose to become one of the most important aspects of globalisation. India's influential role in the production and distribution of spices had a direct impact on the development of globalised economies. As the exchange of spices increased, so did the fortunes of many countries and traders, leading to unprecedented wealth and progress for many nations. Indian spice trade therefore played an essential role in the rise of globalisation.

"The Spice trade has been a symbol of India's resilience and adaptability"

ꕤ

IX

Climate Change and the Indian Spice Trade

The history and significance of the Indian spice trade is an intricate part of the world's past. For centuries, merchants and explorers have sought out this corner of the world for its abundant production of exotic spices, particularly the prized pepper. The Indian spice trade has taken on even greater importance in recent times, however, as the world has become increasingly aware of the looming threat of climate change.

A large part of the spice industry's success is due to the unique climate of India. Unfortunately, due to global warming, temperature swings are becoming increasingly severe and unpredictable. This is putting immense pressure on the spice producers, as extreme temperatures can significantly reduce yield, damage existing plants, and even render certain spices unviable.

Furthermore, climate change is threatening the traditional methods of cultivation used for spices. Specifically, mono-cropping, which once served as a reliable system, is increasingly becoming unsustainable. Because crops are planted in the same spots year after year, the soil is becoming impoverished, causing a dramatic decrease in yields. This means that it is becoming necessary for spice growers to find new methods of cultivation to remain successful.

Finally, climate change is impacting the livelihood of many of the people in the spice industry. Rising temperatures and changing growing conditions have been linked to increased illnesses, as well as other impacts on health. In addition, drought and flooding caused by climate change threaten the security of communities that are dependent on the agricultural industry.

The Indian spice trade is facing many difficult challenges due to climate change, and it is imperative that the international community takes action to address the problem. Governments must implement policies that promote sustainable farming practices, while also working to support communities impacted by the changing climate. If the right measures are taken, it might be possible to ensure the future of the Indian spice trade for generations to come.

"The spice trade has been a catalyst for cultural exchange and globalisation"

ᗢ

X

The Indian Spice Trade Today

Spices have been integral part of the Indian culture for centuries, and India has historically been the world's largest exporter of these essential ingredients. The Indian Spice Trade is alive and well today, with numerous centres all over the country.

India's spice trade is heavily regulated by the Food Safety and Standards Authority of India, which sets standards for quality, hygiene, and product labeling. Participants of the trade must adhere to these regulations to ensure high-quality products.

The Indian Spice Trade has its roots in the fabled spice routes – ancient trade routes between India and the Middle East. Over 5000 years ago, Indian merchants established trading posts along their chosen route and transported a variety of spices to their destination. The demand for

Indian spices was so strong that it even influenced the spice-seeking adventurers of the 16th century.

Today, the Indian Spice Trade is one of the largest markets worldwide, with products ranging from dried spices to fresh herbs and seasonings. The country is the world's largest producer of spices, supplying over 70% of the world's spices, and on average accounts for 15-22% of the global spice trade.

Indian spices are exported to more than 150 countries and regions. The major importers include USA, Middle East countries, the EU and the United Kingdom, South East Asia, and Central Asia. Indian spices are renowned for their flavour and quality, giving them a competitive edge over other spices.

In addition to traditional trading routes, the Indian Spice Trade has been growing rapidly due to the emergence of online platforms. Online traders have quick access to market prices, making it easy to find the best deal on a variety of spices. The ease of access also encourages traders to explore new markets, which has led to a significant rise in the number of participants in the Indian Spice Trade.

The rise of social media has also contributed to the growth of the Indian Spice Trade. Consumers are now able to connect directly with local spice traders, enabling them to discover new flavours, get tips on how to use spices, and even purchase products directly from the source.

Overall, the Indian Spice Trade is a booming industry. With the help of modern technology, an ample selection of products, and a strong customer base, the spice trade remains an integral part of India's economy. Indian spices will continue to influence the cuisines of the world for many years to come.

"The spice trade has been a window to India's diversity and pluralism"

ꕥ

XI

The Future of the Indian Spice Trade

The Indian spice trade has a long and rich history that dates back to antiquity. For centuries, Indian spices have been traded across Asia and Europe, and even today, Indian spices remain some of the most popular and widely used gastronomic ingredients in the world. This makes the Indian spice trade an incredibly important industry to consider for its future development.

In the future, it is highly likely that the Indian spice trade will continue to remain competitive and successful despite increased competition. This is due to the versatility and demand of Indian spices. From traditional curries, to sweeter dishes such as chai lattes, Indian spices are arguably some of the most commonly used in the world. Furthermore, it is likely that as Indian cuisine becomes increasingly popular in the West, the demand for these spices will continue to grow. This in turn could lead to potential innovations in the production and packaging of these spices, so that they can reach the greatest number of people around the world.

Furthermore, Indian spices are incredibly versatile and have the potential to be used in countless combinations and recipes, making them attractive to a wide range of consumers. It is likely that over time more and more diverse uses for Indian spices will be discovered, expanding their already impressive range of uses. Additionally, as health trends continue to focus on natural ingredients, it is also likely that the demand for spices such as turmeric, cinnamon and cardamom will continue to increase.

In order to capitalize on the future potential of the Indian spice trade, it is important that producers and traders focus on marketing their spices in an appealing and modern way to a global audience. This could involve collaboration between producers, better packaging, and an increased focus on innovation. Furthermore, it is likely that firms should take advantage of more digital methods of marketing, such as influencer marketing, to reach a wider audience. This could help to further increase the popularity of Indian spices, and increase the industry's global reach.

Overall, the future of the Indian spice trade is bright, and with the right focus on marketing and innovation it is likely that it will remain competitive and profitable for years to come. As such, it is important for producers and traders to keep abreast of any new developments, and stay up to date with new trends as they emerge. With the right attention, the future of the Indian spice trade is sure to be a highly successful one.

"The spice trade has been an integral part of India's history and culture for centuries."

ꕥ

OTHER BOOKS OF THE AUTHOR

1. The Moments When I Met God
2. Kashiyile Theertha Pathangal
3. GURU GYAN VANI
4. Abhiprerak Gita
5. ASSI SE JAIN GHAT TAK
6. Hopelessness of Arjuna
7. The Soul and It's True Nature
8. Sense of Action (Karma)
9. Action through Wisdom
10. Action through Wisdom
11. THEORY AND PRACTICAL OF EVERY ACTION
12. LOGICAL UNDERSTANDING OF THE SUPREME
13. THE IMPERISHABLE SUPREME
14. Yatra Nishadraj se Hanuman Ghat Tak
15. Yatra Karnatak Ghat se Raja Ghat Tak
16. Yatra Pandey Ghat se Prayagraj Ghat Tak
17. Yatra Ranjendra Prasad Ghat se Dattatreya Ghat Tak
18. YaatraSindhiya Ghat se Gwaliar Ghat Tak
19. Yatra Mangala Gauri Ghat se Hanuman Gadhi Ghat Tak
20. Yatra Gaay Ghat Se Nishad Ghat Tak
21. MAA GANGA, GHATEN EVM UTSAV
22. Ganga Arti Dev Deepavali evam Any Utsav
23. Potentials of Digitalized India
24. VEDIC CONSCIOUSNESS
25. A Brief Introduction to Vedic Science
26. Kashi ke Barah Jyotirling
27. IMPACT OF MOTIVATION
28. Let's have a Milky Way Journey
29. Color Therapy in a Nutshell

30. Rigveda in a Nutshell
31. Yajurveda in a Nutshell
32. Samveda in a Nutshell
33. Atharva Veda in a Nutshell
34. Ayushman Bhava - Ayurveda
35. Srimad Bhagavad Gita and Upanishad Connection
36. Srimad Bhagavad Gita - an attempt to summarize each chapter.
37. Facts and Impact of Nakshatra
38. Astro Gems - NAVARATNA
39. Ekadashi - A Concise Overview
40. A Concise View of Hanuman Chalisa
41. Inspirational Gita
42. Nakshatraranyam
43. Summary of 18 Mahapuranas
44. Synopsis of 18 Upa Puranas
45. Rigvediya Upanishads
46. Shukla Yajurvediya Upanishads
47. Krishna Yajurvediya Upanishads
48. Samavediya Upanishads
49. Atharvavediya Upanishads
50. The Seven Great Sages
51. From Rocket Scientist to President Dr. APJ Abdul Kalam
52. The Visionary's Voice - Quotes of Dr. APJ Abdul Kalam
53. The Wisdom of Swami Vivekananda: Insights and Inspiration from a Legendary Spiritual Teacher
54. Ayurvedic Remedies from the Garden
55. Sages and Seers
56. Rising Strong – Motivational Stories of Women
57. Beyond Flames -Mystery stories of Funeral Ghat Manikarnika
58. The Origins of Tulsi: A Look at the Mythological Roots of the Plant"

59. The Holistic Cow: A Look at the Physical, Spiritual, and Cultural Importance of Cows in India
60. Arts of Healing
61. Exploring the Divine
62. Understanding Five Elements
63. The Etymology of Ram
64. Symbols of India
65. Voice of Change (About Speeches of Great Men)
66. She Speaks (About Speeches of Great Women)
67. Patriotism on Celluloid – Brief About Patriotic Films
68. The Music of Motivation: A Brief Guide to Inspirational Film Songs
69. **Unlocking the Secrets of the Dashopanishads**
70. A Cultural Mosaic
71. Ancient Traditions, Modern Minds
72. Ecos of Ancient Wisdom
73. Beneath the Surface
74. From Temples to Ashrams
75. Sages of the Subcontinent
76. The Art of Healling (Ayurveda, Yoga & Naturopathy)
77. Indian Kitchen
78. The Festivals of India
79. The Indian Epics Retold
80. The Power of Mantras
81. The Indian River Ganges
82. The Indian Architecture
83. Rites of Passage
84. The Indian Silk Road
85. The Indian Literature
86. The Indian Villages
87. The Indian Folks & Crafts
88. The Way of Buddha
89. The Ramayan of Tulsidas

90. Astrological Remedies
91. The Secret Power of Motivation
92. Secret of Developing your Inner Strength
93. The Secret Path to Motivation
94. The Art and Secret of Positive Thinking
95. The Secrets of Practicing Ethical Living
96. Indian Art and Painting
97. The Indian Herbalism
98. Bharatanatyam to Kathak
99. Exploring India's Astrological Remedies
100. The Indian Festival of Flowers
101. Indian Handicrafts
102. The Splashes of Joy – India's Colour Festival

Contact

DR. JAGADEESH PILLAI

PhD in Vedic Science

Four Times Guinness World Record Holder

Winner of Mahatma Gandhi Vishwa Shanti Puraskar and Global Peace Ambassador

Gemology, Astro & Vastu Consultant - Spiritual Counselor

Consultant for designing World Record Ideas

Efficient Tarot Card Reader

9839093003

myrichindia@gmail.com

drjagadeeshpillai@facebook

drjagadeeshpillai@instagram

jagadeeshpillai@youtube

www. JAGADEESHPILLAI.com

|| LOKAHA SAMASTHAHA SUKHINO BHAVANTU ||

9 798889 517092

Printed by Libri Plureos GmbH in Hamburg,
Germany